A BLUE BANNER
BIOGRAPHY

Kate Hudson

Jennifer Torres

P.O. Box 196
Hockessin, Delaware 19707
Visit us on the web: www.mitchelllane.com
Comments? email us: mitchelllane@mitchelllane.com

Mitchell Lane PUBLISHERS

Printing   2   3   4   5   6   7   8

Blue Banner Biographies

Alicia Keys	Allen Iverson	Alan Jackson
Ashanti	Ashlee Simpson	Ashton Kutcher
Avril Lavigne	Bernie Mac	Beyoncé
Bow Wow	Britney Spears	Christina Aguilera
Christopher Paul Curtis	Clay Aiken	Condoleezza Rice
Daniel Radcliffe	Derek Jeter	Eminem
Eve	50 Cent	Gwen Stefani
Ice Cube	Jamie Foxx	Ja Rule
Jay-Z	Jennifer Lopez	J. K. Rowling
Jodie Foster	Justin Berfield	**Kate Hudson**
Kelly Clarkson	Kenny Chesney	Lance Armstrong
Lindsay Lohan	Mariah Carey	Mario
Mary-Kate and Ashley Olsen	Melissa Gilbert	Michael Jackson
Miguel Tejada	Missy Elliott	Nelly
Orlando Bloom	Paris Hilton	P. Diddy
Peyton Manning	Queen Latifah	Rita Williams-Garcia
Ritchie Valens	Ron Howard	Rudy Giuliani
Sally Field	Selena	Shirley Temple
Tim McGraw	Usher	

Library of Congress Cataloging-in-Publication Data
Torres, Jennifer.
    Kate Hudson / by Jennifer Torres.
        p. cm. — (A blue banner biography)
    Filmography: p.
    Includes bibliographical references and index.
    ISBN 1-58415-381-4 (library bound)
    1. Hudson, Kate, 1979 — Juvenile literature. 2. Motion picture actors and actresses — United States — Biography — Juvenile literature. I. Title. II. Series.
PN2287.H74T67 2005
791.4302'8'092 — dc22   2005004243

ISBN-10: 1-58415-381-4   ISBN-13: 9781584153818

ABOUT THE AUTHOR: Jennifer Torres is a freelance writer and newspaper columnist based in Central Florida. Her articles have appeared in newspapers, parenting journals, and women's magazines across the country and Canada. She has written several books for Mitchell Lane including *Eve*, *Ashanti*, *Ashton Kutcher*, and *Paris Hilton*. When she's not writing she enjoys spending time at the beach with her husband John and their five children, Timothy, Emily, Isabelle, Daniel and Jacqueline.
PHOTO CREDITS: Cover — Todd Plitt/Getty Images; pp. 4, 6, 8, 17, 21, 25 — Globe Photos; pp. 12, 28 — Kevin Winter/Getty Images; pp. 13, 18 — Steve Granitz/WireImage; p. 16, 11 — Getty Images; p. 22 — RJ Capak/WireImage; p. 24 — Arnaldo Magnani/Getty Images; p. 27 — Carlo Allegri/Getty Images.
PUBLISHER'S NOTE: The following story has been thoroughly researched, and to the best of our knowledge, represents a true story. While every possible effort has been made to ensure accuracy, the publisher will not assume liability for damages caused by inaccuracies in the data, and makes no warranty on the accuracy of the information contained herein. This story has not been authorized nor endorsed by Kate Hudson.

PLB2,18,29,30

CONTENTS

Kate Hudson inherited her mother Goldie Hawn's fair skin and flowing blonde hair. Her all-American good looks are a welcome addition on the big screen.

A Star from the Start

"**H**ey, watch me sing this song!" yelled the little girl with curly blond hair. "Hey, watch me!" She said again, this time a little bit louder.

Eight-year-old Kate Hudson was trying very hard to get her mother to look at her. The place was filled with people, and everyone was so busy that no one heard her demands. But she knew if she was loud enough she would get noticed.

And she was right. After taking her place on top of a crate, little Kate gathered her breath and thunderously repeated: "Hey, watch me!"

Her mother, movie star Goldie Hawn, glanced over and smiled widely as she gathered the little girl in her arms. Then she sat down to watch Kate do her little song and dance. When Kate was finished, the whole room clapped.

Goldie was filming the movie *Overboard*, but her daughter Kate was stealing the show. And that was just fine with Goldie.

As a little girl, Kate loved to be in the spotlight. She always knew she wanted to follow in her mother's footsteps and become an actress.

"Katie's a spectacular person. She had talent from the beginning," said Goldie.

From the time she was tiny, Kate Hudson felt right at home on a movie set.

She was born just before her mother's big hit movie *Private Benjamin* was in the movie theaters.

At one year old she was a regular on the set of *Private Benjamin*. At two, she kept her mother company on the set of *Best Friends*. Then at four years old she played with other actors' kids on the set of the movie *Protocol*. And at five she joined her mom on the sets of *Swing Shift* and *Wildcats*.

Running around the set, Kate made everyone laugh. But just like the name of the movie her mom was currently filming, sometimes she went a little "overboard."

"Kate was not a quiet, subdued child and she was running around the set," said Garry Marshall, who was directing the movie.

"I used to hold her and say, 'Come on, let's say 'Action' together for mommy!'"

Then Kate and the director would yell, "Action!"

"Oh yeah, I grew up on a movie set," Kate said when she was older. "I'd go to work a lot with my mom, but it wasn't anything glamorous. There was always so much energy on the sets. I remember my favorite time was on the movie *Overboard* because there were lots of kids and it felt like summer camp. Whenever I finished being tutored, I'd help out. I was always in the makeup trailer or I was in wardrobe, or I was helping the camera guys. I never grew tired of it."

It seemed as if acting was simply in her blood.

"My mom says I've been a performer since I was in her womb," said Kate. "I shot out of her belly like a little fireball, ready to conquer."

> *"My Mom says I've been a performer since I was in her womb,"* said Kate. *"I shot out of her belly like a little fireball, ready to conquer."*

Garry Marshall, who has directed many movies over the years, including *The Princess Diaries*, had a case of déjà vu when he filmed *Raising Helen* in 2004. That's because his leading lady this time around was none other than Goldie's daughter, Kate Hudson. The same little girl who had run around his set at the age of eight was now twenty-four years old and the star of his movie.

"I kept calling her Goldie by mistake on this film," said Marshall. "But then they're so similar. They both have this great sense of humor."

Yes, over the years, Kate had gone from watching in the wings to performing before the camera. And now she was the one being watched by the world.

Kate spent much of her childhood on movie sets. She loved watching her mother act and she even got to help the director yell "Action!"

Famous Family

Kate Garry Hudson was born on April 19, 1979, in Los Angeles, California.

Even though Kate recalls a very normal childhood, it was still very different from most. Her parents, Goldie Hawn and Bill Hudson, were celebrities. Her mother was well known for her comical and often zany roles in the movies. Her father was a musician as well as a comedian. They had married in 1976 and had a son that same year. They named him Oliver Hudson. Three years later Kate came along. But the marriage between her parents didn't last, and they were divorced when Kate was only one year old.

After the divorce Kate and Oliver didn't see their father very often. Usually when parents divorce, the kids still see both of them a lot, just at different times. But this divorce was different because her father was different.

"He wasn't really in our lives very much," said Kate. "I didn't know him really well. I didn't understand it. My brother didn't understand it. He was sort of in and out of our lives."

When Kate was three years old, her mother met Kurt Russell, who was also a famous movie star. Kate and Oliver loved him immediately. Luckily for them, so did their mother. The two soon became a couple.

> **When Kate was three years old, her mother met Kurt Russell. . . . Kate and Oliver loved him immediately; so did their mother.**

In time Kate began to think of Kurt as her father. This made Kurt very happy.

"He is my dad," she says of the actor, whom she lovingly calls Pa. "He was always there, for the soccer games, the recitals—always."

When Kurt joined the family, he wasn't alone. He had a son named Boston Russell from a prior relationship. And soon, there was another little one in the house. Goldie and Kurt had a baby boy, and they named him Wyatt Russell.

Together they formed a very happy family. And unlike many other celebrity parents, Goldie and Kurt did not leave the children in the care of others. When they had movies to make, they took turns. That way one parent was always home with the kids.

"My pa was the kind of dad who woke up, took the kids to school and watched CNN all day," said Kate. "Believe it or not, my mom still knits and reads. It was all so very normal." She continued, "My parents were very

Kate's husband, Chris Robinson (far left), was welcomed into Kate's big family, which includes her brothers Wyatt Russell (middle) and Oliver Hudson (far right), her mother Goldie Hawn, and her "Pa" Kurt Russell.

careful not to bring their work home and they didn't throw big raving parties. They're not those kind of people."

Kate's home was filled with lots of love. And even though her parents could afford to buy her anything she asked for, they didn't spoil her or their other children. All the kids had chores, did homework, and played school sports. They grew up with a deep respect for hard work and the importance of family.

"I laugh when people go on about the advantages I have—my mother's main influence has come from just being a great parent," said Kate. She did not grow up with all the latest toys or a pony of her own. She had to earn the things she had. Her parents wanted her to learn respect for her things.

Kate recalls, "I was very lucky because we were never spoiled as kids. One of the big things growing up was that my parents were adamant about us understanding how lucky we were. We never got any perks. My parents challenged us to do our chores and by not giving us expensive things without working for them."

But being the child of Hollywood royalty did have its perks. Kate got the chance to meet a lot of other famous people, and her mom was able to take her to work with her whenever she wanted to.

As Kate grew older she knew she wanted to be an actor like her parents. She loved everything about the movies. And she was determined to make her dream of fame a reality.

Kate graduated from Crossroads School for Arts and Sciences and was also accepted at New York University's Tisch School of Drama, but instead of going to college, she decided to jump right into acting.

Even though Kurt Russell isn't her biological father, Kate always thought of him as her "Pa."

*Kate's mother, Goldie Hawn, takes her job as a mother very seriously.
Her children, Kate, Oliver, and Wyatt, (shown here) always come first.*

The Road to Fame

Many people think it's easy for someone with famous parents to find work as an actor. But that isn't always true.

Kate may have gotten auditions, but with her famous last name, most directors in Hollywood wouldn't take her seriously.

That's why when Kate decided to try out for her first film at the age of seventeen, she didn't use her real name. It was a role for the movie called *Escape from L.A.* It starred her Pa, Kurt Russell. He had told Kate that she should try out, but she told him she wasn't ready. The truth was that she was going to try out, but she wanted to get the role on her own.

The day of the audition, she drove herself to the studio. She had made sure Kurt wasn't going to be on the set. It was all in her hands now.

After Kate tried out for the movie, she went home and waited to hear about the part she knew she had won.

That call never came.

Kate didn't get the part.

The setback didn't discourage her. She was sure she was meant to be a Hollywood star, so she kept going on auditions.

Later that same year, she won a role on an episode of a television show called *Party of Five*. It was very popular in the late 1990s. It also had a very young cast. The show was about five siblings (brothers and sisters) who are left to find their own way in the world when their parents are killed by a drunk driver.

Kate's character's name was Cory. Everyone thought she did a great job. The part was for only one episode, but it was a good start.

> Kate was not about to give up. She knew she would make it if she just kept trying. She was glad her parents taught her not to be a quitter.

More auditions came and went. Kate was not about to give up. She knew she would make it if she just kept trying. She was glad her parents had taught her not to be a quitter.

Then a couple years later, she got her big break.

She was asked to costar in a movie. The movie had a very strange name: It was called *200 Cigarettes*.

The exciting part was that it starred some of her favorite Hollywood actors, including Christina Ricci and Ben Affleck.

Acting came naturally to Kate, who first appeared in a small role in the critically acclaimed movie 200 Cigarettes, *which also starred Ben Affleck (left) and Jay Mohr (right).*

Kate was very happy. This was what she had been waiting for. The chance to show her talent was before her. She wasn't about to fail.

Kate worked very hard on the film. When it came out in the movie theaters, people loved her work. Many wondered why she looked so familiar. It wasn't until later that many people found out she was Goldie Hawn's daughter.

Kate and Goldie are told they look alike all the time. Both have long, curly blond hair. They are the same height. And they both have the same laugh.

After *200 Cigarettes* was released, more good things began to happen.

Kate was cast in several films, including the thriller *Gossip*. But her breakthrough role was just around the corner.

Kate was cast in the movie *Almost Famous*, the Cameron Crowe follow-up to *Jerry Maguire*. The film got rave reviews.

Kate's star was rising fast.

Kate's role in Almost Famous *earned her rave reviews. The movie did well at the box office, and Kate's work in the film earned her an Oscar nomination, the most important award an actor or actress can receive.*

Kate in a scene from the movie Almost Famous.

When Kate Hudson met Chris Robinson, it was love at first sight, and the couple soon wed. However, by summer 2006, they were splitting up.

A Star is Born

*I*n *Almost Famous* Kate played the role of Penny Lane. The movie is about a rock band and their fans. Kate's character is a fan. She played her role so well, she won a Golden Globe Award and was nominated for an Oscar. The Golden Globe is a very important award in Hollywood. It means you are respected. The Oscar is the biggest award an actor or actress can be given. She didn't win the Oscar, but being nominated was an honor that meant she was now a real "star."

Movie offers started pouring in.

She starred in three more movies over the next three years. They were *Dr. T and the Women, The Cutting Room,* and *Four Feathers.*

Directors really wanted Kate in their movies! She was becoming very popular. Kate was even offered the chance to play Mary Jane Watson in *Spider-Man.* But she turned it down. The role later went to Kirsten Dunst. *Spider-Man* was a huge hit. Kate said she turned it down on purpose. She knew it would be a blockbuster. She said just wasn't ready for "big-time" fame.

But there was another reason.

Kate's life had taken a big turn. She had met Chris Robinson. Chris was a musician. He had been part of a popular band called The Black Crowes. He started another band, Chris Robinson and the New Earth Mud.

> Kate's life had taken a big turn. She had met Chris Robinson. . . . Kate and Chris fell in love. They married on the last day of 2000.

Kate and Chris fell in love. They married on the last day of 2000.

Goldie and Kurt were very happy.

"Chris likes to make my mom laugh and my mom likes to make Chris laugh," said Kate.

The young actress decided she needed to take a break.

Her mother told her, "Go be a wife for a little bit because it will be the best thing you ever did."

Kate took her advice.

"I was really tired," said Kate. "I thought, I'm only 21 years old and I'm exhausted. I was so happy and everything had been so high energy that at the end, everything kind of dropped off. I said I needed to sleep for three weeks—and it turned into a year."

Even though it may seem that actors have an easy life, the work can be hard. Long days and nights spent doing a scene over and over can wear you out. Kate loved every bit of it, but she knew when to take a rest.

After her break, Kate got back to work. She went full steam ahead. She filmed three movies: *Alex & Emma*, *Le Divorce*, and *Raising Helen*.

While filming *Le Divorce*, she and Chris traveled to Paris, France. They took their two dogs along. One of them was named Clara. Most nights Clara the Pomeranian would join the couple for dinner at a restaurant. In fact, Clara ate right off their plates. In Paris it's normal to let your dog eat out with you!

"Clara loved it there. Her tail was up the whole time," said Kate.

Finally Kate and Chris came back to the United States.

Kate was set to star in another movie. It was called *How to Lose a Guy in 10 Days*. The movie was a comedy, and she had fun on the set. While filming it, Kate got some big news. She was pregnant!

Kate appeared in the movie Raising Helen *in which she was left to care for three children after her sister and brother-in-law were killed. Having her own children was something Kate dreamed of doing.*

Kate Hudson and Matthew McConaughey starred together in the movie How to Lose a Guy in 10 Days. *While filming the movie, Kate found out she was pregnant.*

Kate was so excited. This was something she had wanted very much.

Chris and Kate got ready to have the baby.

The baby wouldn't arrive for about eight months, so Kate kept filming her movie. When the movie came out in theaters, it was a box-office hit. In fact, the movie made more than $100 million in ticket sales!

Now it was time to wait for the baby's arrival.

"I can't wait to bring a little human being on to this planet," said Kate. "It will be the most beautiful thing in the world."

A New Beginning

On January 7, 2004, Ryder Russell Robinson was born. He was a healthy 8 pounds, 11 ounces. Kate was happier than she had ever been.

"I can't begin to describe what this means to us as a couple," said Kate. "We were in love before but this has taken it to a new level. It's the best feeling we've ever felt being together."

Little Ryder got his name from one of his father's songs.

"I went to see Chris on tour near the end of my pregnancy," said Kate. "Every night they would end with the song 'Ride.' So it was like, 'Let's call him Ride.' And later that became Ryder."

When Ryder was just a few minutes old, Kate told Kurt Russell that she had a surprise for him.

"I remember being rolled out of the surgery room right after I had him and I looked up at my pa and I said, 'Did you meet Ryder Russell?'"

Since Russell was Kurt's last name, he was very flattered.

Kate and Chris named their son Ryder Russell. The name Ryder came from one of Chris's songs. The name Russell was a tribute to Kate's "Pa" Kurt Russell.

As a new mom, Kate hoped to be as good as her own mother and Pa.

"They're my role models as a parent," said Kate. "I can only hope that when Ryder and the next kids come, they like me as much as I like my mom."

And Kate wants more kids. Lots more! But that would have to wait, at least for a little while. It was time to think about acting again. Three months after Ryder's birth, she would be filming the movie *The Skeleton Key*.

This movie would be a little different from the others. It was a mystery. Like her mother's career, most of Kate's work had been in comedies. As always, Kate was up for the challenge.

She began an exercise program and ate a healthy diet to get back in shape. Kate lost the weight she had gained while pregnant.

Kate continues to challenge herself in her acting. The suspense movie The Skeleton Key *gave her the chance to show her more dramatic side.*

"I did it gradually which was important," she said. "I didn't want to suddenly drop the weight drastically. It was hard work."

But hard work is something Kate likes. She enjoys a challenge. Being secure in herself allows her the freedom to make mistakes and grow stronger.

> **Hard work is something Kate likes. She enjoys a challenge. Being secure in herself allows her the freedom to make mistakes and grow stronger.**

Even though she's a star, Kate remains very "normal." Kate plays the banjo and the guitar. She also loves to knit and make arts and crafts.

In 2003 Kate was listed as number 99 in *Premiere* magazine's Power 100 List. It was her first appearance on the list, and at the age of twenty-four, she was the youngest person on it that year.

"It's a nice place to be when you're young, to feel secure in your life and your career," said Kate. "For the moment, it's a beautiful thing."

Her brother, Oliver, has also gone into show business. He has acted in a number of movies. He also starred in the 2004 TV series *The Mountain* and appeared in several episodes of *Dawson's Creek*.

Kate is proud of her brother and calls him a real "hunk."

As for Kate, the future is very bright. She is young. She is a Golden Globe winner. Her name is well known across the world. Directors love to work with her. They say she is a very nice and friendly person. Her movie-star status didn't

At times, Kate Hudson looks almost identical to her mother Goldie Hawn at the same age. They have both been to the Golden Globe Awards many times.

change her kind personality. So the movie offers keep coming. She is constantly on magazine covers. When she walks down the red carpet, she is one of the best-dressed women around.

Life is good for Kate. It's good because no matter what happens to her career, she knows she will always have her family. And family is the most important thing in the world to her. No amount of money can replace a loving family.

As she raises Ryder, she remembers her own childhood with happiness. Kate knows that being rich or famous doesn't make someone happy. It's all about the love in your

Kate believes in the support and love of family. She had a happy childhood, and she hopes to raise her son Ryder with the same kind of love and affection she received when she was growing up.

life. And Kate has a lot of love around her. It's a love she shares every day with her son and the rest of her family.

Most nights she and her husband, Chris, sing and play the guitar to little Ryder. They spend all the time they can with him — just as her parents did with her when she was young.

"My parents are an inspiration when it comes to parenting," said Kate. "I had a wonderful childhood thanks to them. And that's what I can hope to pass on to Ryder, that sense of being loved like that. That's the most important thing."

CHRONOLOGY

1979   Kate Garry Hudson is born on April 19 in Los Angeles, California, to parents Goldie Hawn and Bill Hudson.

1980   Kate's parents divorce; she has limited contact with her father.

1984   Goldie Hawn and Kurt Russell meet on a movie set; Kate begins to think of Kurt as her father.

1996   Kate wins her first role on the television show *Party of Five*.

1997   Kate graduates from Crossroads School for Arts and Sciences and is accepted at New York University-Tisch School of Drama.

2000   The movie *Almost Famous* is released to rave reviews; Kate marries rocker Chris Robinson.

2001   Kate wins a Golden Globe Award for Best Supporting Actress for her role in *Almost Famous*. She is also nominated for an Oscar.

2003   Kate is ranked No. 99 in *Premiere* magazines' Power 100 List.

2004   Kate and Chris's son, Ryder Russell Robinson, is born on January 7.

2005   Kate appears in a ONE commercial, a campaign to help support people in poverty; Kate reads diary entries of young people during the Holocaust Documentary "I'm Still Here" airs on MTV (USA); the movie *Skeleton Key* is released.

2006   Kate and Chris separate after six years of marriage.

FILMOGRAPHY

2006	*You, Me and Dupree*
2005	*The Skeleton Key*
2004	*Raising Helen*
2003	*Le Divorce*
	Alex & Emma
	How to Lose a Guy in 10 Days
2002	*The Four Feathers*
2001	*The Cutting Room*
2000	*Dr. T and the Women*
	Almost Famous
	Gossip
	About Adam
1999	*200 Cigarettes*
1998	*Ricochet River*
	Desert Blue

FOR FURTHER READING

Book

Modifica, Lisa. *Goldie Hawn and Kate Hudson (Famous Families).* Rosen Publishing Group, 2004.

Articles

Degen Pener, "Great Kate," *In Style*, August 2003.

Lawrie Masterson, "Great Kate," *Sunday Mail*, Queensland, Australia, May 30, 2004.

"Kate Hudson Knows 'How To,'" CNN Entertainment Online, February 11, 2003. http://www.cnn.com/2003/SHOWBIZ/Movies/02/11/wkd.fiveqs.kate.hudson.ap/

"Kate Hudson Profile," *Hello* magazine. http://www.hellomagazine.com/profiles/katehudson/

Martyn Palmer, "Raising Helen Star Kate Hudson Talks About Baby Son and Grandma," *The Mirror*, August 27, 2004.

"Raising Helen: Motherhood Role Hits Home with Star Kate Hudson," *Kate Hudson Heaven*, May 27, 2004. http://www.broken-tears.org/kate/kate/press sunsentinelmay2704.php

Rebecca Thomas. "Kate Hudson; More than Famous," *BBC News*, February 9, 2001. http://news.bbc.co.uk/1/hi/entertainment/1160641.stm

Tiffany Rose, "Film: I've Been a Performer Since I was in the Womb." *The Independent* (London), August 13, 2004. http://enjoyment.independent.co.uk/film/interviews/story.jsp?story=550762

Vicki Woods, "Sparkling Star," Sassysara.com. Enter BBO - click on Ladies - Kate Hudson - Info - Articles - Magazine Articles - Vogue 2002.

INDEX